Iceland Travel Guide

Thomas Leon

Iceland Travel Guide

ISBN-13: 978-1548792817

ISBN-10: 1548792810

First Edition: July 2017

10 9 8 7 6 5 4 3 2 1

Thomas Leon

CONTENTS

Introduction

First off, kudos on making the decision to visit one of the most picturesque countries you will ever see. Indeed, my first impression of Iceland left me completely spellbound: from the wild, untamed moors that still bears traces of the Viking

Age to the numerous hot springs, volcanoes and endless adventures, this is world that's as diverse as you can get. Yes, there are unpronounceable names and yes, it does get awfully cold in the winter, but this is one country that I would absolutely recommend to anyone.

A seasoned traveler, I have seen my share of wonderful sights from all around the world but there was something about Iceland that fascinated me right from day one. This is why, in this book, I will provide you with descriptive and up-to-date information that will help you turn you trip to Iceland into the best ever vacation.

Hike with me through majestic glaciers, where time will literally feel like it's come to a complete standstill.

Join me in my quest of chasing the elusive Aurora Borealis in the dead of winter and learn everything about Iceland's stunning Midnight Sun that will provide a one-of-a-kind vacation to tourists visiting in the summer.

If you ask me, there are very few places in the world that can provide so many adventures in one single vacation.

In this book, I'll also give you an idea of what to expect in terms of food, both gourmet and budget-friendly.

Worried that you won't be able to afford proper accommodation in Iceland? Fret not: I'm also taking you across a list of some of the best luxury resorts, hotels, hostels and rental cottages in the country, all of which are suited to different budgets.

And if you want to indulge in some shopping (which of course you'll want to do!), follow me as I show you where to get the best bargains and value for your money.

So grab your warm clothes, hiking boots and- of course- this book as you embark upon a lifetime's worth of adventures in one single vacation to Iceland.

Chapter 1: Practical information

Should you get a tour guide?

Whether or not you choose to go with a tour

3

guide/pre-set package largely depends on your sense of adventure and direction as well as your budget. Personally, I did have a guide for most of my Icelandic adventures, but I also did enjoy the times I went around on my own. The main advantage with getting a tour guide is- obviously- that you'll end up saving both time and money instead of trying to find your way around an entirely familiar land on your own and often ending up where you're not supposed to! Basically, a guide will help you save various vacation time since you won't be constantly getting lost or trying you find your way around.

On the flip side, some guides can be expensive, especially if you're not going out with a large group. Still, if you ask me, it's worth forking out for a guide all to your own. There's nothing I hate more than large-scale, commercially-oriented guided tours and I would strongly recommend that you stay away from those, especially in a country like Iceland, where there's just so much to discover. Indeed, the major con to guide tours is that you'll need to go ahead with a preset schedule, even if it means getting up at 5am just so you can start off your day at 6am.

Planning your Icelandic trip on your own- or with an individual guide- can be quite liberating in the sense that you'll get to do exactly what you want, nothing more, nothing less. If you want to experience the Midnight Sun, be sure to visit in July, when the sun never truly sets!

Getting around Iceland

Because Iceland is a relatively small-scale country, it's quite easy to get around, especially during the summer when bus run their full schedule. From Reykjavík, you can catch a bus- or even a flight- to different regions of the country. The only practical way to travel from North to South Iceland in the winter is undoubtedly by flight since most buses only run for a few hours in the morning. The best thing about Iceland is that, being one of the most popular holiday destinations in the world, it is extremely easy to rent four-wheelers, camper vans and cars, most of which are protected by solid insurances. If you're on a restricted budget and don't have a lot of distance to cover, you can also rent bicycles or scooters.

During summer, several private bus companies over long-distance shuttles around Iceland. Out of the four major companies, three are based in Reykjavík: Sterna, SBA-Norðurleið and Strætó. These bus companies cover the Westfjords as well as Iceland's Ringroad and through the Interior. If you're trying to stick to a budget, though, be warned that as convenient as they are, buses in Iceland can be quite expensive. For example, I paid around 15,500 ISK (one way) to travel from Reykjavík to Akureyri, before quickly finding out that flying was actually cheaper in some cases.

Whether you choose to travel by bus or planes, it's important to book in advance. Most of the interior routes that are covered by private bus tours departing from Reykjavík include Lakagígar,

Mývatn, Askja, the bare strikingly desolate Sprengisandur route as well as the picturesque Kjölur route.

Best time to visit

Again, this depends on your personal preference (and how well you can withstand the cold, of course), but having visited Iceland both in summer and winter alike, I would have to say that I much prefer the Icelandic summer. Bear in mind that this is no tropical vacation though: the weather does remain fairly unpredictable, even in the summer where temperatures can reach around 17 degrees Celsius, with the occasional misty and wet spells. I also experienced days where the temperature will go down to 9-10 degrees Celsius smack in the middle of summer.

Most attractions are only open during those warmer months which run from late May to early/mid-September. In the winter, you will certainly experience stinging cold with a climate that fluctuates between minus 7 to minus 8 degrees C. Daylight is severely limited, with most attractions and establishments open until around noon. When I was stayed in Reykjavík during the winter, I was quite stunned to see sunsets at 1pm. Memorable experience, yes, but definitely not practical if you want to explore your new surroundings.

What to bring

If you're visiting in the winter, you'll definitely need ski jackets, mufflers, thick gloves, hats, extra socks, waterproof boots and the likes. But if you're heading to Iceland over the summer, your suitcase will certainly be lighter.

Here's what I bought when I went to Iceland during summer:

- Waterproof shoes

- Waterproof jacket

- Fleece Jacket

- Long-sleeve shirts

- Hiking shoes/boots

- Jeans

- Tights and/or leggings

- Gloves

- Hat

- Winter jacket

- Shawls or pashminas

Chapter 2: The Hidden Wonders of Iceland

Along with the usual touristy areas, Iceland is one country that holds its fair share of hidden wonders, some of which I got to explore thanks to my native friends.

When visiting those lesser-known areas of Iceland, caution is always the key. Remember that you'll be heading off to some remote, desolate terrains so be sure not to wander about with a lot of money and valuable items. Iceland is actually a pretty safe country and I've never had any negative experiences there, but it's always best to be vigilant. You'll also need fully-charged cell phones, spare batteries, torches and a GPS app (or an old-fashioned map) as you head off on your journey to uncover those hidden gems.

I would also strongly suggest a solid 4WD to visit these areas since you will encounter more than your fair share of gravel roads, most of which are still unpaved. A 4WD can also come in handy when visiting mountain roads. Don't neglect insurance protections either: you will want a solid travel insurance plan as well as gravel insurance. And of course, do check out the weather forecast before heading off to remote areas, even if you're travelling in the summer.

One last thing: Don't forget your selfie sticks and waterproof cameras: believe me, you will need them!

The Highlands

If you've ever wanted to experience what it- literally- means like to be smack in the middle of nowhere, you'll certainly want to check out Iceland's interior Highlands, where no human has ever set up a permanent home. In fact, the interior highlands doesn't even receive as many visitors as other parts of Iceland, hence providing you with a unique chance to experience nature in its most vibrant, rawest form. Oases of vegetation, dormant and active volcanoes alike, hot springs, glacial moraine and extended stretches of black sand await you in this truly intriguing part of Iceland.

Here are some of my favorite things to explore in the Highlands.

Discover exquisitely carved calderas

Believe me when I say that the profound sense of isolation combined with a deep, heavy silence that covers the Highlands do make for a life-changing experience. This region is also home to the world-famous Askja Volcanic Area, which is basically a tight circle of nested calderas (cauldron-like features that closely resemble craters). A rare and unique sight, these calderas were formed after the land collapsed prior to a particularly violent volcanic eruption. Standing in the middle of the Askja Volcanic Area is no different than how it might feel like to stand on an alien planet: vast, desolate and made up of lava, ash and rainfall. In fact, astronauts preparing for the Apollo lunar programs often visited Askja to mentally prepare themselves for what to expect on the moon.

Take a hike through Thorsmork Nature Reserve

Another popular attraction in the Highland is the Thorsmork Nature Reserve, named after Thor, the Norse hero. One of Iceland's most popular hiking areas, this reserve has been protected by the Forestry Service since 1922. Because it is surrounded by three massive glaciers, this region tends to be slightly warmer than other Highland areas. In fact, you might even come upon greener areas filled with birch wood, fern and moss. Near this Nature Reserve, you will also find one of the world's coldest rivers known as the Krossa.

Kverkjokull glacier: Ice caves and more

Deeper within the interior Highlands is the

Kverkfjoll volcano and mountain ranges, which has been split into two by the Kverkjokull glacier. I was nothing short of captivated by the splendor of this majestic valley punctuated by vivid hues of green, black and red. The mountain ranges conceal hot magma chambers underneath, which actually created several intricately carved glacial ice caves in the region. Because this region has quite a high altitude as it stands at 900m above sea level, the air is quite thin so you need to be relatively fit to explore it. The Highland's highest peak stand at 1936m and is found on the eastern range of the Skarphédinstindur Mountains.

I would highly recommend that you hire a tour guide to take you around Iceland's desolate Highlands. While visiting the Highlands was one of my favorite Iceland adventures, there's no denying that you do need an experienced guide to guarantee your safety, considering how remote and desolate these areas are.

The Southern Coast

From roaring cascades to stunning glaciers, Iceland's Southern Coast holds plenty of wonders that are bound to please just about anyone, whether you're travelling solo or with your friends and family. When I first visited the Southern Coast, I have to say that I was literally stunned into silence by the exquisite vistas that stretched out at my feet. If you ask me, there are very few places on earth that can come close to rivalling the glorious beauty that makes up Iceland's Southern Coast.

Brace yourself for a bumpy ride

I'll be honest with you though: you do need to cross an extremely bumpy and frankly quite uncomfortable mountain road before you reach the Southern Coast, so it may not be the best place for you to visit if you easily get car sick. My journey was punctuated by alarming bumps and humps, resulting in someone from our group getting quite violently sick. However, if you can survive the first portion of the journey, rest assured that as soon as you cross the Hellisheiði Mountains, it's quite a smooth drive towards the South Coast.

Unleash your adventurous bone with a challenging Glacier Walk

Let me start by emphasizing that glacier walks across the south coast are best suited to tourists who are in excellent physical conditions. The first time I took a glacier walk, I was quite unprepared by how painful and stiff my joints would be the following day. Kudos to my guide, Tony, for bearing with me as I painstakingly struggled to catch up with the others.

Still, if you're ready for a challenging activity, I would strongly suggest taking a glacier walk across Iceland's scenic Southern Coast. Several agencies offer tours, complete with guides, ice axes, crampons, helmets and other types of safety equipment. The price can range between 9500 and 10,000 ISK and the walk can take up to 5 hours. Available all year round, most of these adventures start from Sólheimajökull glacier.

Experience extreme beauty at Landmannalaugar

While Iceland is undeniably one of the most stunning countries I've ever visited, the sights that I saw at Landmannalaugar were seriously out of this world. Boasting unvarnished beauty, this mountainous area is bursting with a variety of minerals, resulting in an impressive medley of colors. Thanks to Landmannalaugar's volcanic origins, you will be able to explore hot springs as well as old lava fields. There's even a camp area for visitors, where my group and I set up tents for the night. Believe me when I say there's nothing like waking up to the pure, unfiltered mountain air. And you won't even need to worry about food since there's a mountain shop near the camp where you can buy water, tea, coffee as well as different types of Icelandic delicacies that you can buy for breakfast or dinner.

Best of all, if you visit Landmannalaugar during the summer (which I would highly recommend since the weather's nearly unbearable in the winter!), you can even try your hand at fishing in one of the many lakes that surround the region, which incidentally, is known for its abundance of mountain trout. I will admit though that we are all pathetic fishermen but thankfully enough, our ginger-haired guide Kari, managed to catch a couple of trout which we roasted over a campfire. If you want to take things to the next level and visit the area like the Vikings once did, you can also rent a couple of horses in the region and gallop across endless stretches of black sand.

Explore the translucent pools at the Westfjords

If you're under the sad illusion that you need a bit of luck to spot one or two hot springs in Iceland, think again. Ironically dubbed "the most famous unknown place in Ireland", the Westfjords house a truly impressive collection of hot springs and translucent pools. And yes- you can totally swim in them! Just be extremely careful to dip just the tip of your toe in first to check the temperature: while all of the springs that I tested were pleasantly hot, some can be hotter than others so you should definitely proceed with caution.

Some of the top sights in the Icelandic Westfjords- other than the geothermal pools of course- include:

The Djnjandi Waterfall- or Iceland's Jewel

Locals call it the Jewel of Iceland. And after seeing it with my own eyes, I have to agree. I scrolled through quite a few travel pictures before heading off to Iceland, but I have to say, as stunning as those pictures were, none of them prepared me for the wondrous sight that greeted me as I stood in front of the Djnjandi Waterfall. Cascading an impressive 99 meters, this waterfall has often been compared to a bridal veil because of its luster and beautiful ripples as it tumbles into the pool below. What sets it apart from most other waterfalls is that it starts off with a width of 30 meters and gradually opens up until it has a width of around 60 meters by the time it reaches the surface of the pool.

Even the route towards Djnjandi is nothing short of scenic: with an elevation of approximately 200 meters above sea level, I have to say I was quite enthralled by the bird's eye view of Iceland that greeted us as we made our way to the top. If there's a way to see as much of Iceland as possible in one trip, this certainly is it. And of course, you can always take a plunge into the wonderfully clear pool at the bottom of the waterfall- yet another reason to visit the place in summer!

Check out the adorable Artic animals at The Arctic Fox Center

A non-profit exhibition center with a particular interest in foxes, this Center was one of the (many) highlights of my trip to Iceland. The arctic fox is actually the only terrestrial mammal that is native to Iceland. First established in 2007, this center is open all year long and is an absolute must-see if you're travelling with kids. Along with different exhibitions, this place also includes cafes, Cultural Centre as well as a Tourist Information Centre. If you're feeling particularly adventurous, you can also book a kayak tour not far from the center and leave all your troubles behind as you glide on the smooth Icelandic waters.

Tomato Farms and More

If you dare venture deeper into Iceland, you will certainly uncover the type of hidden destinations that are- at least till date- virtually unknown to the majority of tourists. Most of them are easily accessible by car and you can either book a guide with your car rental or embark upon your own self-drive tours, armed with only a map and an excellent sense of adventure!

Here are just a few of the places that honestly made me want to move to Iceland permanently!

The Grótta Nature Reserve

Entirely natural, the Grótta reserve is abundant with a generous birdlife and is considered by the locals as the best place to enjoy the afternoon sun as it dips low beneath Faxfloi Bay. Best of all, this reserve houses one of Iceland's most exclusive hot spring which is notoriously hard to find- unless you know it's there, of course. Nestled among the rocks that border the sea, this little pool enables you to enjoy the soft crash of the waves against the shoreline as you relax in its abundant warmth. Nearby, you will also find an absolutely picturesque lighthouse that will once again appeal to your sense of adventure: indeed, this lighthouse is only accessible during low tides which means that you only have three hours to reach there and three hours to return. Take any longer and you'll be forced to spend the night right there at the lighthouse until the tide goes down again. Fun, eh?

Friðheimar tomato farm for a stunning eating experience

Located in the South of Iceland in the world-famous Golden Circle, Friðheima is the kind of organic tomato farm that will make you feel as though you're in a far-away corner of Naples. Personally, we visited this family-owned establishment during lunchtime, having heard that it's the perfect spot for a light bite to eat during the day. After wolfing down half of what was on the restaurant's menu- and topping it off two scoops of tomato ice cream (far more delicious than it sounds!), we were taken for a tour of the tomato and cucumber fields.

A lunch of Tomato soup with homemade cinnamon bread, cucumber salsa, Bloody Mary and of course- the famous tomato ice cream- only cost around 1900 ISK for three people, which was quite a bargain considering it also included a free tour of the premises.

Rauðisandur beach: An out of this world sight

Iceland is certainly known for its black beaches, but did you know that there's one particular beach that actually presents acres of red sand? Indeed, the magnificent clash between the scarlet shoreline and the turquoise waves that await you when you set foot on Rauðisandur beach is nothing short of amazing. A lesser-known fact is that this clash of colors actually provide plenty of optical illusions: depending on the position of the sun, you can actually see the sand turn yellow, orange or white in front of your very eyes.

Because it is completely deserted, this is the ideal spot where you can enjoy long walks to clear your head as you inhale that wonderfully pure, salt-tinged sea breeze to refresh your senses. In fact, you can walk all the way towards Látrabjarg cliff at the far end of the beach, where you will be able to admire clusters of puffins from afar.

To reach this beach, you can either drive across the Westfjords or else board a ferry directly from Stykkishólmur. If you opt for a self-drive tour, be sure to hire a 4WD because driving on this beach can be extremely tricky, especially during winter.

Spend a night on Flatey Island

This island is yet another part of Iceland that's still relatively unknown to tourists. If you do get the chance to visit though, it's definitely worth spending the night. Because cars are not allowed on the island, you will be treated to spectacular nights, unblemished by light pollutions, punctuated by the roar of the waves crashing against the shore. To reach the island, you can board the Ferry Baldur from the bay of Stykkisholumur.

If you don't want to spend the night, rest assured that the ferry does make a three hour stop over there, but come on- why wouldn't you want to spend at least one night on this picturesque island? Described by the locals as a place where time stands still, Flatey Island does come with a single hotel. You won't even have to worry about overbooking because of the few number of tourists who actually know about the place. This Icelandic land has one single main road that will take you down to the scenic village where you will be able to see houses and small buildings that date all the way back to the 19th century. You can't help but have a distinct impression that you've somehow travelled back in time as you stroll through the stone-paved streets, visiting historic sites and ancient libraries. I can certainly attest to the sense of stillness that locals told me about before I headed off to Flatey; almost as though time holds absolutely no meaning on this charming island.

Chapter 3: Icelandic Adventures

If you don't have the time to chase after Iceland's many hidden jewels, rest assured that the traditional touristy adventures are just as exhilarating. One of the things I absolutely adore about Iceland is that I always get to embark upon the type of adventure that I most certainly won't be able to do elsewhere in the world! From experiencing the sublime sense of peace and tranquility that comes with the Blue Lagoon or taking a scenic drive across the Golden Circle, believe me when I say that Iceland will appeal to your sense of adventure like no other place.

So buckle up as I take you through some of the most memorable- and popular- adventures in Iceland!

Admire the Northern Lights

Head over to Iceland during the winter for this one. Believe me, the cold and the wet and the long nights will be completely worth it! And yes, contrary to popular belief, it is entirely possible to view the elusive aurora borealis in Iceland- if you know where to go.

The first thing to know is that you need the proper viewing conditions to stand a chance of seeing the Northern Lights, which is why it's best to head away from the city lights if you can. Granted, there have been a couple of instances when the aurora borealis were seen glowing and shimmering in the sky above the capital, Reykjavík, but this is quite a rare occurrence. However, if you don't have a car to get out of Reykjavík, fret not: one of the ideal places to spot the Northern Lights is from the Grotta Lighthouse which is around twenty minutes away from the capital on foot. If you're staying in Northern Iceland, other places where you can spot the lights include the Thingvellir National Park (which is completely black and deserted at night), Hljomskalagardur Park or near the Perlan, a popular dome-shaped building.

Your bet of seeing the aurora borealis largely increases if you head over to the gothermal region of Landmannalaugar. While it is quite a popular hiking site during summer, this area remains quite desolate during winter, which means that you won't be exposed to any unnecessary light pollution. While there are no buses heading towards Landmannalaugar in winter, you can easily rent your own vehicle. I would (once again) strongly recommend 4x4's since the terrain can get quite rocky and uneven over there.

Personally, I think it's best to book a northern light adventure through an agency in order to save both time and money. When I went to Iceland, I booked a pre-made package that took us all the way to the south coast, on the beach of Vik. There was something almost magical about huddling in front of a campfire on the beach, listening to the mighty roar of the waves as we waited for what our guide promised to be the show of a lifetime. And indeed it was. At nearly one in the morning, the sky suddenly burst into life with glowing waves of vivid greens, pinks and purples. Nothing can actually prepare you for such a display. I'll admit that our tour was quite expensive- most Northern Lights Adventures normally are- but it was worth every cent.

Another popular place to see the Northern Lights in southern Iceland is near the Jökulsárlón Glacier Lagoon, which is around 5-6 hours away from Reykjavík. Be sure to look for deals online since some agencies offer dual Northern Lights and Glacier Hiking adventures.

Take an Icelandic Cruise

Whether you choose to board a cruise directly from Iceland, or travel there from your part of the world, rest assured that there are plenty of companies that offer Iceland cruises at varying rates. Here are some of the highest-rated cruises where you will be able to fully immerse yourself into the world-famous Nordic culture.

Iceland- Between Geysers & Glaciers

Organized by Le Soleal, this 8-day cruise departs from Iceland and will take you right to the very edge of the Arctic Circle, where you will be able to follow the exact path the Vikings took way back in the 9th century. This is the ideal cruise for anyone who wants to explore a kaleidoscope of romantic and wild landscapes, punctuated by boiling geysers, volcanoes, vertiginous fjords and massive glaciers.

Three Arctic Islands

A 14-day cruise aboard the Ocean Nova is anything but boring. Quite on the contrary, this ship will take you all the way to Scorsbysund which is located on Greenland's northern coast. Following this, the Ocean Nova will take you around Iceland before moving on to Spitsbergen, which is considered as the highest point of the Arctic Circle. This Icelandic cruise is your best bet if you want to spot elusive animals such as walruses, reindeers, musk oxen as well as polar bears. A personal favorite of mine, this particular Icelandic adventure does admittedly cost more than the average cruise, but it's also extremely diverse, enabling you to visit several destinations in the same vacation.

Jewels of the Arctic

This 14-day expedition onboard the Polar Pioneer combines the raw beauty of Iceland, Greenland and Norway. This particular Icelandic cruise will treat you to exceptional sights in the likes of fjords, icecaps and- if you're lucky- maybe even a berg or two. The best thing about this cruise is that if you book during winter, you can largely increase your chances of spotting the Northern Lights.

Spitsbergen- East Greenland- Iceland

Another multi-destination Icelandic cruise,

this adventure takes place onboard the Sea Spirit and is considered to be quite affordable for a 15-day trip. I would suggest this particular trip if you want to visit a couple of Arctic destinations before finally arriving in Iceland for your vacation. On this cruise, you will be able to explore the world's largest and most popular fjord system in East Greenland before visiting the unearthly glaciers of Iceland.

Circumnavigation of Iceland

If you want to explore Iceland's intricate geology, there's no better way than to take a Circumnavigation of Iceland cruise onboard the world-famous National Geographic cruise ship. Best of all, you will be able to benefit from the opinions of the many experts onboard the ship as you explore boiling mud pots, cliffs, thundering waterfalls and more. This 360 degree expedition also includes regular lectures onboard and if you're lucky, you can even follow some of the professional National Geographic photographers as they work on their latest projects. This expedition normally lasts for 9 days and run from June to July every year.

Drive across the Golden Circle

If you ask me, the Golden Circle is what put Iceland on the map. Easily the most popular tourist route in southern Iceland, this area joins Reykjavík to the southern uplands of the country. This is the route that will take you across some of Iceland's more scenic tourist spots such as the world-famous geysers Strokkur and Geysir as and many more.

The best way to visit the Golden Circle- at least in my opinion- is by your own rented 4-wheeler. The best thing about driving yourself around this region is that you get to control exactly how long you spend in each place, without being burdened by a pre-conceived schedule which mainly includes quick stops every here and there. But then again, if you don't feel like driving all day, you can also book one of the thousands of tours that take tourists across the Golden Circle on a daily basis. Because it is such a popular tourist attraction, you certainly be will spoilt for choice when it comes to selecting your very own Golden Circle tour.

Some might say that a full day of driving is not enough to cover the entire Golden Circle- and I agree. Personally, my group and I thought it would be best to spend the night at a quaint hotel in Gullfoss before resuming our adventure the following day. You can also find several summer cabins in this region.

The Gullfoss Waterfall

This is truly one of my favorite places in

Iceland and a tourist spot that I would absolutely recommend to anyone, especially if you're a nature lover. With plenty of glorious photo opportunities, this regions houses the massive Hvítá River that tumbles down to create Gullfoss, one of the most iconic, three-step waterfalls in the world. Because it is one of Iceland's most popular excursions though, be ready to face large crowds, especially if you visit during those peak summer months.

Þingvellir National Park

Established in 1930, the Þingvellir National Park once used to house Icelandic Parliamentary sessions before being turned into an absolutely breathtaking park to mark the 1000th anniversary of the Althing. Because of its natural wonders and diverse flora and fauna, this particular park was declared a World Heritage Site in 2004. In this park, you will also find the famous Silfra canyon, which is also an absolutely stunning diving site. Fans of geology will be able to admire from up close the faults and cracks that dot the path, pointing towards the continental drift that once occurred between the Eurasian Plates and North America.

Take a dip in the Blue Lagoon

According to the locals, a trip to Iceland isn't considered complete without a visit to the most famous geothermal spa in the world, the Blue Lagoon. I have to admit I wasn't overly excited at the prospect of heading off to a spa when I was all geared up for a thrilling adventure. But boy was I surprised when I agreed to follow my group- albeit grudgingly- to the Blue Lagoon. Forget the traditional beige-carpeted spas with soothing music in the background: this spa is actually located on a lava field in the Reykjanes Peninsula, which explains the presence of minerals such as sulfur and silica in the water.

Be advised though: the Blue Lagoon receives thousands of visitors each year, if not more, so to avoid any unfortunate surprises, it's always a good idea to book way at least a few days in advance.

Your skin will thank you

Upon arrival, we were informed that thanks to the mineral-rich waters, bathing in the Blue Lagoon has been shown to be extremely beneficial to the skin, even helping with those hard-to-treat conditions such as psoriasis. Best of all, the massive pools are naturally warm, with a temperature that ranges between 99-102 degrees F. In fact, because of the water's proven capabilities, the Blue Lagoon even houses a development and research facility that focuses on finding cures for other types of skin conditions, using this very same water.

Because of its strict code of hygiene (which of course, I was extremely grateful for!), guests have to shower in the changing room, where they will be handed a robe before being admitted to the swimming area. And don't worry: you're not gonna just float around either. Bars have been set up right into the pool, so you can sip on a gloriously chilled Icelandic beer as you unwind in the warm, steaming water. Beauty bars are also available right in the water, where you can choose from different types of face masks that you can smear over your skin to maximize the benefits of the mineral-rich water and steam. And I can attest to the fact that I did emerge from the lagoon with visibly clearer and smoother skin.

Guests younger than 15 years old do need to be accompanied by a guardian before entering the lagoon. For an extra fee, you can also rent bathing suits, towels and additional bathrobes. You can also book extended tours that include flights from different corners of Europe, hotel stays and entry to the Blue Lagoon.

Experience the Midnight Sun

A phenomenon unique to Arctic regions like Iceland, the Midnight Sun is undeniably something that everyone should experience at least once in their lives. To witness this truly magnificent natural wonder, you should head over to Iceland during summer: in some cases, the midnight sun can start as early as May- or as late as August, for that matter. My first day (and night) under the midnight sun brought on a blend of excitement and complete bewilderment: while it does feel several very, very long days devoid of any night whatsoever, your internal clock will kick off at your usual bedtime, regardless of how bright it is outside. For this reason, virtually every hotel in Iceland are fitted with thick blackout curtains during summer.

The best thing about the Midnight Sun? It literally doubles the number of hours you'll have to experience the very best that Iceland has to offer. My favorite sunlit night activities included- but were by no means limited- to:

Reykjavik Dance Festival

If there's one thing the people of Reykjavik are famous for, it's their all-night parties. Yup, this is one country that knows how to throw a week-long bash. Which is exactly the capital organizes a yearly dance festival that's normally held during those sunlit nights between August 25 and August 30. This is when you will truly get to experience Icelandic culture at its rawest: from local treats to artisanal music, here's your chance to dance all night long under the sun!

The Arctic Open

Often held in mid-June, the Arctic Open will enable to you to participate in a game of midnight golf at the prestigious Akureyri Golf Club. First established in 1986, this tournament offers visitors the chance to enjoy incomparable quiet and peace as they tackle a 36-hole course over two days. If you feel like you can rise to the occasion, you can also try your hand at the more challenging 18-hole championship that stretches across 6,400 yards of greenery.

Secret Solstice Festival

Okay get ready for this. Not only are you gonna party under the midnight sun, but you're going to party smack in the middle of the Langjökull glacier! According to the locals, the

Secret Solstice Festival is actually the only party in the entire world that's held in a glacier. This festival only admits 100 people though so be sure to get your tickets way in advance.

Chapter 4: Accommodation in Iceland

Regardless of your budget, you'll undoubtedly find a charming and- more importantly- comfortable place to sleep during your Icelandic vacation. But then again, if you can afford to splurge, then by all means go for a luxury resort. The majority of luxury resorts in Iceland also come with geothermal spas where you can enjoy some of the most invigorating treatments in the world.

Enjoy some much-needed pampering at Hotel Rangá

This 5 star resort specializes in Northern Lights Vacation packages, but also offers wonderfully comfortable and highly luxurious accommodation all year round. A mere hour away from Reykjavík, this hotel is far enough from the city lights to present you with a spectacular show of the aurora borealis, but close enough for you to indulge in some shopping and general sights of the city. Because the entire hotel is design to shroud you in a lap of luxury, most bathrooms have even been fitted with whirlpool baths where you can relax for as long as you want after a full day of exploring Iceland.

All the rooms are equipped with a minibar, coffee and tea maker, hairdryer, bathrooms and slippers and even free WiFi. Guests of the hotel can additionally benefit from a 24 hour room service as well as customized room decoration. Boasting a log-cabin style, this hotel is anything but stuffy, in spite of its exquisitely meticulous service and elegance: get ready to see stools shaped like female buttocks, towering statues of polar bears and other such cheeky accents. Indeed, very few establishments can offer such a seamless blend of refinement with the occasional humorous touch to provide you with the perfect vacation in Iceland.

While this is one of the most luxurious hotels in the world, you will be able to see the owners virtually every day: Fridrick, the owner and Ingiphor, the manager, are always on field, ready to greet the guests and offer some highly-valued travel tips. As far as the services are concerned, Hotel Rangá offers an in-house restaurant with local and international dishes alike, golf course, laundry facilities, bar, and of course, the spa where you can pamper yourself for as much as you'd like. The hotel can even take you on a variety of Icelandic adventures that include snowmobiles, diving, river jets, hiking trips, ATV Motorbikes and the likes.

One of my favorite features at the Hotel Rangá is their customized rooms: indeed, their luxury suites are each themed after one of the seven continents. Along with the suites, guests can also choose from a variety of equally comfortable rooms, most of which face the Mt. Hekla volcano or the East Ranga River.

If it is luxury that you're after, other such Icelandic resorts include Hotel Grimsborgir, Hotel Edda ML Laugarvatn, Radisson Blu Saga Hotel and Hotel Borg by Keahotels, among many others.

Budget-friendly accommodation in Iceland

On the other hand, if you're travelling on a smaller budget, rest assured that you can choose from an extended variety of hostels, guesthouses and even cottages. While some of these establishments are self-catering, the majority do come with a restaurants where you can enjoy some Nordic treats like Reindeer steaks and more.

Hotel Laxnes, for example, is a family-owned establishments that's ideal for anyone who wants a budget-friendly room without compromising on comfort. Indeed, this hotel boasts Northern Lights and Mountain facing views, 7 self-catering studios with cooking facilities, 13 double rooms, 2 family rooms as well as 3 suites. With several free WiFi hot spots, this hotel even boasts a hot tub which faces the mountain Esa. Thanks to the on-site pub, you will be able to enjoy different types of local drinks without having to head off to town. In spite of its affordable prices, this hotel additionally offers airport transfers as well as a plethora of guided tours and activities that will enable you to soak in that unique Nordic culture. Examples include Sea Fishing with Barbecue lunch, Northern Lights, Snafellsnes, South Coast & Jökulsárón Glacier Lagoon tour, among others.

Another budget-friendly Icelandic accommodation- and a personal favorite of mine- is the Bakki Cottage located on the Northern coast of the country. This charming cottage overlooks the wild Nordic ocean, which is ideal for anyone who wants to experience nature at its best. Equipped with two bedrooms that can hold three beds each, this self-catering cottage also comes with a fully-equipped kitchen with various appliances, coffee makers, microwave, fridge and hot plates, among others. Best of all, a geothermal hot tub has also been installed on the partially-covered veranda, which also comes with barbecue facilities and outdoors furniture.

If you're looking for a hostel, you can also check out the KEX. Located in an ex-biscuit factory, this particular establishment offers a wide range of facilities in spite of being one of the least expensive accommodation in Iceland. From laundry rooms to an in-house gym or a fully stocked kitchen where you can prepare your own meals, guests can enjoy a plethora of amenities designed to render their stay even more comfortable. If you don't feel like cooking, you can also enjoy a variety of delectable meals in the hostel's gastro pub, which boasts some of the best home cooking in Iceland. Every morning, you can enjoy a varied breakfast buffet and in the evenings, you can mingle with the hostel owners, locals and your fellow guests over pints of local beer.

As far as the rooms at the KEX hostels are concerned, guests can choose from different types of rooms including shared dorms as well as guesthouse-style, double and single bedrooms that boast their own private bathroom. If you're travelling with your family, you can make the most out of the family rooms that can sleep 4 to 6 people while accommodating a baby crib. If you do want to enjoy a touch of luxury, you can also splurge for the Double Room Plus which is a spacious bedroom styled just like a hotel. This room overlooks the mountain and you will also benefit from additional amenities such as housekeeping and daily breakfast in beds.

Chapter 5: Eating in Iceland

If you're not used to it, Nordic food can, at times, feel drastically different from your usual fares. If you ask me, Iceland is the absolute best place to experience the very best of Nordic food because of its diverse culinary culture. Instead of simply sticking with your hotel's restaurant, do take the time to explore some smaller family-owned eateries where you might be pleasantly surprised by the thrilling blend of flavors.

I'll be honest with you though: as experimental as I am when it comes to cuisines from around the world, I couldn't bring myself to try the traditional Icelandic delicacies such as hrutspungar (Pickled ram testicles) or hákari (Shark meat. Served rotten. Literally). Yeah, sounds delicious, I know.

Fret not, though. Other than these...exotic (for lack of a better word!) delicacies, Iceland does boast several more traditional dishes which are an absolute delight for the palate. One of my personal favorites is Pylsa- a sort of hot dog with a Nordic twist, served with dried onion, sweet mustard and smothered in a special Icelandic sauce known as remolaði. Served in a traditional hot dog bun, this delicious little snack is available in just about any gas station.

Another popular fast food in Iceland is dried cod fish, served cold in pre-packaged sachets. Okay, I have to admit: the thought of opening a Ziploc bag to feast on small pieces of cold dried fish does not exactly sound appetizing. But trust me on that and give it a try. It might just be the most delicious thing you'll ever taste in your life.

And while we're on the subject of food in Iceland, it's important to know that the cuisine hasn't changed much since the Viking Age so there's plenty of seafood and various types of meats on the menu. Minke whale is considered a delicacy in the area- with locals constantly having to reassure tourists that no, Minke whale is not an endangered species in Iceland. It is commonly served seared, skewered or in steak form, with dollops of the famous Icelandic Skyr. A cross between soft cottage cheese and yogurt, Skyr is an absolute staple in Iceland: locals consume it literally at any time of the day. As healthy as it is, Skyr also tastes wonderful, like a unique blend of soft-serve ice cream, whipped cream and Greek yogurt.

With that brief overview of Icelandic staples in mind, read on for a list of the best places to eat in the country.

Budget-friendly restaurants: Eat like the locals

Café Babalu

Its warm vibe and quirky décor makes it one of the most uplifting cafes that I've ever been to. I use the term café loosely though: this establishment actually spans over two levels. With several local snacks that can easily constitutes as meals, and a wide range of coffees and teas available, it's the ideal place to warm up after a cold hiking day. If you're planning on visiting this Reykjavík-based establishment a try, do give the house soup a try. You can thank me later!

Ostabúðin Fish and Soup

Another restaurant located in Reykjavík, Ostabúðin Fish and Soup once used to be a cheese shop but gradually spread its wings to become one of the most popular eateries in the capital. Like the locals proclaim, this is where you'll get the best fish in all of Iceland. Best of all? They have daily specials for lunch, where you can enjoy delectable albeit affordable dishes.

Noodle Station Soups

The best joint in town for soups and noodles, as well as noodle soups, this charming little establishment offer 3 kinds of soups- vegetarian, chicken and beef. Patrons can add their own spices into their bowls and most of the dishes rarely exceed 1180 ISK.

Vegamót Bistro

Extremely popular among the locals, this bistro is great for a Friday night out. With dishes made from the freshest of produce, meat and fish, this bistro is also known for its innovative menu with new items constantly being added to it. A full meal could set you back around 200 ISK, which is quite an excellent deal for a centrally-located bistro.

Gourmet restaurants for refined palates

Grillmarkadurinn

This gourmet restaurant might be on the more expensive side but believe me when I say it's absolutely worth it. The chefs work closely with local farmers and fishermen to ensure that your meals are made with the freshest of produce. This is the place to be if you want to sample Nordic twists on quail, trout, beef, lamb, skyr and even honey. One of the chefs, Guðlaugur P. Frímannsson, even holds a Michelin star. A few of my favorite dishes at this restaurant include the Fish Gourmet Plate (combination of cod, redfish, salmon served with vegetables and garlic potatoes), Langoustine Tails served with champagne sauce as well as their own twist on the Straweberry Pavlova. If you're not sure what to get, you can even go for the Tasting Menu that consists of small portions from various items on the dinner menu.

Kol Restaurant

Kol Restaurant and Bar is especially renowned for its craft cocktails and comfort cuisine which has traditional Nordic twists on classic dishes. Between them, head chefs Kári Þorsteinsson and Einar Hjaltason have over 20 years of experience in fine dining. This restaurant is particularly known for its 3-course set menu which includes Risotto with lemon confit, tiger prawns and parmesan followed by Charred Salmon cooked medium rare and served with dill potatoes, fennel, dill hollandaise and apples as well as a White Chocolate Cheesecake served with liquorice parfait, granola as well as fresh passion fruit. For an added fee, you can indulge in a delicious wine pairing. A few other specialties include their Vegan Nut Steak, Breast of Duck and Rillet, Sautéed Ocean Pearch and Langoustine and Mussels in Broth, among others.

Kopar

Located in the capital, Kopar is yet another gourmet restaurant where you will be able to sample the very best that Iceland has to offer in terms of food. A few of my favorite items off the starter menu include Blueberry Cured Beef Tenderloin served with caramelized walnuts and parmeggiano, creamy Rock Crab soup as well as Green Salat, which includes pickled cucumbers and olives in lemon oil. As for their main courses, patrons can choose Mussels & Crispy Sweet Potato Fries as well as different types and preparations of fish.

Icelandic street food

When you're visiting Iceland- or any other country for that matter- never hesitate to check out the different stalls and street vendors to sample local food at its freshest. Iceland street food is extremely diverse and chances are, you'll probably get to try the kind of delicacies that you won't find in restaurants or cafes. Below are a few of the most popular street food in Iceland:

- Icelandic hot dogs

- Fish tacos

- Icelandic meat soups with mutton, rice and potatoes

- Subs served with a variety of sauces

- Doughnuts served with caramel sauce, cinnamon or chocolate

- Charred sheep's head

- Waffle with whipped cream and strawberry jam

- Lobster sandwiches

Chapter 6: Shopping

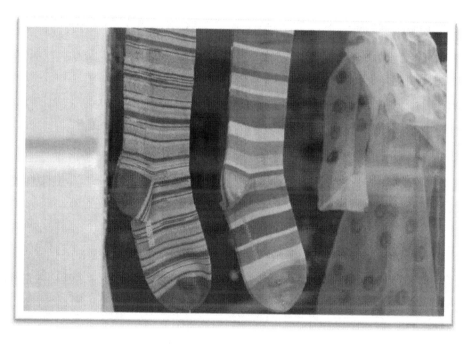

Okay, I'll admit: Iceland isn't exactly known for its shopping. But if you know where to go, you'll certainly be able to head back home laden with souvenirs as well as local crafts and different types of clothes at bargain price. I was actually quite surprised by how affordable haute couture was in Iceland- and I didn't even have to compromise on the quality of the clothes either. In fact, if you plan on shopping for luxury items and brands, I can honestly say that Iceland is one of the best places in the world to do it. Why are these items so cheap there? I have zero idea. But there's one thing I can tell you: I can never turn down a good bargain. And you'll certainly find plenty of those in Iceland.

Best places to shop in Iceland

As the country's capital, Reykjavík undoubtedly offers the best shopping opportunities: in fact, the best thing I liked about shopping there is how close the stores are to each other. Since they were all within walking distance of my hotel, I was able to save precious vacation time by going from store to store on foot, instead of having to wait for the to travel long distances. Don't hesitate to check out the capital's famous 'Wash Road', where you can find several clothes and home accessories stores at affordable prices. Even if you don't plan on doing any shopping, the Wash Road is worth a visit since it's considered to be one of the coolest and most brightly decorated roads in the whole of Iceland.

Tourists who want to invest in outfits that refer Iceland's quirky culture should definitely check out the Laugavegur's fashion scene. Kiosk, for example, is a medley of eight local designers who specialize in silk shirts, printed leggings and digitally printed knitwear sporting artsy designs. Another one of my favorite places to shop in Iceland is the Kringlan Shopping Centre: quite popular among locals and tourists alike, this mall is flanked by other historic buildings such as the State Broadcasting Service, the City Theatre as well as the House of Commerce. Close enough to the majority of hotels, this particular mall offers more than 80 shops that spans across two levels- basically enabling you to do all your shopping in one place. In addition to its extensive number of shops, this mall also boasts a plethora of services and entertainment such as the 'Land of Adventure' for kids, photo exhibitions by local artists as well as local musicians and actors who frequently roam the malls to entertain shoppers. Because it is such a well-loved place, the city even offers free shuttles to this particular mall.

For luxury shopping, head over to Smáralind Shopping Center where you will find local as well as international designer brands such as Diesel, Nike, Pandora, Vero Moda, Apple, TopShop, Dorothy Perkins, Karen Millen, Hugo Boss, Zara,

Dressmann, Esprit and many more. Again, you'll undoubtedly be pleasantly surprised when you'll see the price tags, especially if you compare the value of these same items in European shopping capitals such as Milan. Described as Iceland's most contemporary mall, the Smáralind Shopping Center aims to create a street-like atmosphere with plenty of sunlight, ambient lighting and typical Icelandic architecture. With a plethora of restaurants and no less than 100 shops, this mall also offers a variety of hiking gear that you'll need to hike across glaciers. This is also the place to be for designer jewelry such as Jón & Óskar Goldsmiths, Meba Rhodium and Carat, among many more. In this mall, you'll also find a health club and a spa specializing in traditional Icelandic treatments with mineral-infused geothermal water.

How to avoid common tourist traps

It's not just Iceland: every popular tourist destination in the world has its fair share of tourist traps. Luckily enough, there are quite a few ways of avoiding these traps and getting your money's worth. First off, as much as I love the Icelandic shopping malls, it's worth heading off to the smaller markets, as rundown as they may appear to be. These are actually where I got some of the best bargains, and you can be sure to find just about everything there, from clothes to local crafts, souvenirs, food and more.

As friendly as Iceland is, there are unfortunately a few charlatans who are more than eager to take advantage of unsuspecting tourists by selling fake designer clothes and accessories. The rule of the thumb here is: if it's too cheap to be true, it's most likely a fake. Of course, designer items are less expensive than usual in Iceland, but if you're offered a Prada handbag for $20, rest assured that it's a total scam.

Here are a few tips to avoid the most common scams:

Steer clear of Puffin shops

Yes, once upon a time, Puffin was one of the most prestigious brands in Iceland. Sadly, it has nowadays become a playground for imitations and fakes- most of which are imported from Thailand and China. The alluring Viking Puffin-branded helmet you're itching to bring home is most likely made from plastic.

Near Beer

Cleverly marketed as a special kind of local craft beer without any side effect, this is unfortunately nothing more than highly diluted beer from the cheapest corners of the world. No wonder there's no hangover in the morning since most of the stuff is basically water.

Airport taxis

That's a given in just about any country of the world. Outrageously overpriced, Iceland's Airport Taxis can easily be identified by their yellow signs on the roof. Just to give you an idea of the price, the 60-minute drive from the capital to the airport will cost you around 18,000 ISK while that same journey only costs you around 2200 ISK by bus.

Bottled water

If you have to pay for water in Iceland, it's more likely a scam. Yes, I know how surprising this sounds but Iceland is actually one of the rare countries in the world where water is entirely free. Because of the abundance of H_2O, you can literally ask for a glass or bottle of pure mineral water anywhere you go so avoid paying for it for as much as you can. In fact, for something that's free in the country, bottled water- especially in supermarkets- can be quite expensive. Alternatively, you can walk around with your own bottle and fill it from faucets. Tap water is entirely safe in Iceland.

Traditional souvenirs from Iceland

Hot dog mustard

Yes, I know. It sounds weird. But one bite of Iceland's hotdogs and you'll be begging for more of that mustard sauce. Iceland's mustard is quite different from English, French or the American variety. It's actually a glorious combination of mustard, remouladi and ketchup. Readily available in supermarkets, these plastic bottle of mustards can last for several months.

Reyka vodka

Before you step on your flight back home, do make a stop at the duty free and pick up a few bottles of Reyka vodka. Not only is it cheaper by around 60% than what you'll get in bars, but according to local legend, this vodka is made from a recipe that dates all the way to the Vikings Age.

Blue Lagoon products

Like we've covered before, the bottom of the Blue Lagoon is covered in a variety of rich minerals and silica that has soothing properties for the skin. So if you're visiting this geothermal spa, you can stock up on jars of the silica as well as various types of lotions and face washes to take back home with you.

Books

Yes, I know. Souvenir books are a thing of the past. But I do have a penchant for them, which is only fueled by my obsessive habit of picking up an art book from each country that I visit. The one I bought from Iceland feature a collection of the country's most scenic regions. More importantly, such books will make excellent souvenirs for you to take back home.

Woolen crafts

You can't go to Iceland without picking up a traditional Icelandic sweater. Don't hesitate to go wild on the print either. There's nothing like a puffin-covered sweater to remind you of those wonderful days in Iceland. For the best bargains on sweaters, check out the Kolaportid or even the Thorvaldsens Bazaar where the proceeds are donated to charity.

Lava Rock crafts and Jewels

If you're not one of those tourists who scoop up cans of ashes from volcanic regions, you can always invest in crafts and jewels made from lava rock. Bracelets, earrings, rings and even necklaces made from local volcanic rocks will certainly echo Iceland's volcanic origins.

Conclusion

At the end of the day, if you're still hesitant about your trip to Iceland, I would absolutely recommend you to go for it. Yes, it's cold and yes it's undoubtedly going to be a long-haul flight, but believe me when I say it's worth it. Not only is it diverse enough to provide amazing value for money, but believe me when I say you'll feel like the days are just flying by. Indeed, there's so much to see, so many wondrous sights to take in that even the longest vacation won't feel enough to cover all these adventures.

If you ask me, Iceland is the one place in the world that can so effortlessly blend hours of glorious relaxation with thrilling activities that will set your pulse racing. Of course, you should always take the prerequisite precautions of comparing different hotels and package prices to ensure that you get the very best deal but at the end of the day, rest assured that Iceland will have something for you, regardless of the type of adventure that you want to embark upon. An added bonus? The locals are extremely proud of their Nordic culture and eager to share it with the world which means that you'll mean more than your fair share of friendly locals who will never once hesitate to point you towards the right direction.

And as you stand on the wild moors overlooking the Arctic Circle, with a volcano to your left and glaciers to your right, you will finally realize why Iceland has been dubbed "The Land of Fire and Ice."

Take it from it. It truly is.

Thank you so much for reading this book. I hope it's useful for you.

If you like the book, would you please do me a huge favor and write me a review on Amazon? I would really appreciate it and look forward to reading your review.

Best

Thomas

Check out my travel books...

Hawaii

TRAVEL GUIDE

Thomas Leon

New York

TRAVEL GUIDE

Thomas Leon

Made in the USA
Middletown, DE
28 January 2018